THE CHRISTMAS PORRINGER

EVALEEN STEIN

ILLUSTRATED &

PUBLISHED BY

e-KİTAP PROJESİ & CHEAPEST BOOKS

www.cheapestboooks.com

 www.facebook.com/EKitapProjesi

Copyright, 2019 by e-Kitap Projesi

Istanbul

ISBN: 978-625-7959-25-4

E-ISBN: 978-625-7959-04-9

TABLE OF CONTENTS

CHAPTER 1

KAREN ASKS ABOUT CHRISTMAS

OVER the old Flemish city of Bruges the wintry twilight was falling. The air was starry with snowflakes that drifted softly down, fluttering from off the steep brown roofs, piling up in corners of ancient doorways, and covering the cobblestones of the narrow streets with a fleecy carpet of white.

At a corner of one of the oldest of these and facing on another no wider than a lane, but which bore the name of The Little Street Of The Holy Ghost, a number of years ago there stood a quaint little house built of light yellow bricks. It had a steep gabled roof, the bricks that formed it being arranged in a row of points that met at the peak beneath a gilded weather-vane shaped like an arrow. The little house had no dooryard, and a wooden step led directly from its entrance to the flag-stones that made a narrow, uneven walk along that side of the street.

Icicles hung from the edge of the brown roof and twinkled in a crystal fringe around the canopy of the little shrine up in the corner of the dwelling. For, like so many others of the old city, the little house had its own shrine. It was a small niche painted a light blue, and in it, under a tiny projecting canopy of carved wood, stood a small figure of the Virgin Mother holding the Christ-child in her arms. Now and then a starry snowflake drifted in beneath the canopy and clung to the folds of the Virgin's blue robe or softly touched the little hands of the Christ-child nestling against her breast.

And, by and by, as the wind rose and blew around the corner of the house, it began to pile up the snow on the sills of the casement windows whose small panes of glass lighted the room within, where sat an old woman and a little girl. The woman was clad in a plain black gown, such as is still worn by the humbler of the Flemish dames, and on her silvery hair was a stiffly starched cap of white.

The little girl was dressed much the same, save that her light brown hair was not hidden but braided in two plaits that were crossed and pinned up very flat and tight at the back of her head.

The woman was bending over a rounded pillow, covered with black cloth, which she held in her lap; it was stuck full of stout pins, and around these was caught a web of fine threads each ending in a tiny bone bobbin, and beneath her skillful fingers, as they deftly plied these bobbins in and out, a delicate piece of lace was growing; for it was thus that she earned bread for herself and the little girl.

Indeed, the lace of Bruges, made by the patient toil of numberless of her poorer people, has for many centuries been famous for its fineness and beauty. And those who so gain their livelihood must often begin to work while they are still children, even as young as the little girl who sat there in the twilight by the window of the little yellow house.

She, too, was bending over a black-covered pillow, only hers was smaller and had fewer bobbins than that of the white-capped woman beside her; for the child was just beginning to

[5]

learn some of the simpler stitches. But though the bit of lace on the pillow showed that she had made good progress, she was working now slowly and had already broken her thread twice, for her mind was full of other thoughts.

She was thinking that the next night would be Christmas eve, and that she would set her little wooden shoes by the hearth, and that if she had been good enough to please the Christ-child, he would come while she was asleep and put in them some red apples and nuts, or perhaps—perhaps he might bring the little string of beads she wanted so much. For Flemish children do not hang up their stockings for Santa Claus as do the children of our land, but instead, at Christmas time, they set their little shoes on the hearth and these they expect the Christ-child himself to fill with gifts.

As the little girl by the window now thought and thought of Christmas, her fingers dropped the thread at last and, looking up from her task with her blue eyes full of dreams, "Grandmother," she said softly, "will the Christ-child surely come again tomorrow night? And do you think he will bring me something?"

"Why, yes, Karen, thou hast been a good child," answered Grandmother, who was trying hard to finish a difficult part of her lace pattern before the dark fell.

"And, Grandmother," went on Karen, after thinking a little longer, "is it really his own birthday?"

"Yes, yes, child," said Grandmother.

"Then," said Karen, as a bewildered look crept into her eyes, "why is it that he brings gifts to me, instead of my giving something to him? I thought on people's birthdays they had presents of their own. You know on my last one you gave me my blue kerchief, and the time before, my pewter mug." Karen considered a moment more, and then she added: "Is it because we are so poor, Grandmother, that I have never given the Christ-child a Christmas present?"

Here Grandmother's flying fingers paused an instant, though still holding a pair of the tiny bobbins, as she answered, "It is true we are poor, Karen, but that is not the reason. No one gives such gifts to the Christ-child. Thou must give him obedience and love; dost thou not remember what Father Benedicte told thee? And then, too, thou knowest thou art to carry a wax candle to the cathedral for a Christmas offering at the shrine of the Blessed Virgin and Child."

"But," continued Karen perplexedly, "does *no* one give him something for his very *own?*"

"There, there, child," said Grandmother, with a note of weariness in her patient voice, "I cannot work and answer thy questions!"

And Grandmother bent still closer over the flower of lace which she was trying so hard to finish, and the little girl became silent.

After a while, from the beautiful tall belfry that soared into the sky from the center of the city, the chimes rang out the hour, and, no longer able to see in the gathering dusk, Grandmother rose and laid aside her work.

"Come, Karen," she said, "put up thy work, and get thy shawl and go fetch some water for the tea-kettle."

The little girl carefully placed her lace-pillow on a shelf at one side of the room; and taking a knitted shawl from a peg near the doorway, she ran to the dresser and lifted down a

[7]

copper tea-kettle, polished till it shone. Then she unbarred the door and sped out into the snowy dusk.

She had but a short distance to go to the quaint pump that served the neighborhood. It stood among the cobblestones of the narrow street, and had been made long, long ago, when the workmen of even the commonest things loved their craft and strove to make everything beautiful that their fingers touched. So the pump had a wonderful spout of wrought iron shaped like a dragon's head; and as Karen tugged at the long, slender handle of the same metal, she laughed to see how the icicles hung from the dragon's mouth like a long white beard. She liked to pretend that he was alive and wanting to eat her up, and that she was very brave to make him fill her tea-kettle; for Karen loved fairy stories and lived a great deal in her own thoughts.

Meantime, the dragon had not eaten her, and the copper tea-kettle was brimming over with cold water, seeing which she stooped and lifting it in both hands, carefully carried it back to the little yellow house and set it on the hearth where Grandmother had raked out some glowing coals. Then she lighted a candle, and helped prepare their simple evening meal of coarse brown bread and coffee, though this last was for Grandmother; for Karen there was a pewter mug full of milk.

When they had finished their supper, Grandmother placed her lace-pillow on the table close to the candle and again bus-ied herself with her work. For the wife of Burgomaster Koerner had ordered the lace, and it must be finished and sent home the next day.

And Grandmother sorely needed every penny she could earn; for, since Karen had neither father nor mother, there was no one but herself to gain a livelihood until the little girl grew older and could help carry the burden. To be sure, Grand-mother was not really so old as she looked, but many years of toil over the lace-pillow had bent her back and taken the color from her face. While Karen's father had lived they had known more of comfort; but when he died and the mother had fol-lowed soon afterward, leaving her baby girl to Grandmother's care, there had been but little left with which to buy their bread. That had been eight years before, but Grandmother had struggled bravely on; she was one of the most skillful of the scores of lace-makers of the old city, and so she had managed still to keep the little yellow house in which she had always lived, and to shield Karen from knowing the bitterest needs of the poor.

But Grandmother was weary; and as now she bent over the fairylike web of lace in which she had woven flowers and leaves from threads of filmy fineness, she was glad that the piece was almost finished, and that she would have the blessed Christmas day in which to rest.

And while Grandmother's fingers flew back and forth among the maze of pins, Karen was busy tidying up the hearth and the few dishes which she neatly set back on the old-fashioned dresser near the fireplace. Then she drew a little stool close to the hearth, and, resting her chin on one hand, looked dreamily into the fire.

She was still thinking of Christmas eve, and the more she thought the more she wanted to give something to the Christ-child. For she was a generous hearted little girl and loved to share any little pleasures with her friends, especially those who had been so good to her. And she considered the Christ-child the most faithful friend she knew, "for," she said to her-self, "as far back as I can remember, he has come every

Christmas while I was asleep, and has always put something in my wooden shoes! And to think that no one gives him any present for himself!" For Karen could not see how giving him one's obedience or love (for, of course, every one expected their friends to love them anyway!), or offering a wax candle in the shrine at the cathedral, could take the place of some little gift that he might have for his very own.

Surely, she thought, the Christ-child must like these things just as other children do. If only she had some money to buy something for him, or if only she had something of her own nice enough to offer him! She went over in her mind her little possessions; there was her blue kerchief, her pewter mug, her rag doll, her little wooden stool; but none of these things seemed just right for the Christ-child. And, besides, she felt that he was so wonderful and holy that his present should be something not only beautiful, but also quite new and fresh.

Poor Karen gave a sigh to think she had not a penny to buy anything; and Grandmother, looking up from her work, said, "What is the matter, child?" And as Karen said nothing, "Where is thy knitting?" asked Grandmother, " 'tis yet a little while till bedtime; see if thou canst remember how to make thy stitches even, the way I showed thee yesterday."

"Yes, Grandmother," answered Karen; and going into the little room that opened off from the living-room, she came back with a bit of knitting and again seating herself on the wooden stool, began carefully to work the shining needles through some coarse blue yarn. For little Flemish girls even as young as she were not thought too small to be taught not only the making of lace, but how to knit; and their hands were seldom allowed to be idle.

Indeed the folk of the humbler class in Bruges had to work long and industriously to keep bread on their tables and a shelter over their heads.

The city had once been the richest and most powerful in all Flanders, and up to her wharves great ships had brought wonderful cargoes from all over the world; and the rulers of Bruges and her merchant citizens had lived in the greatest splendor. The wealthy people were wealthier and the poorer people less poor in those old days. But then had come bitter wars and oppression; the harbor had slowly filled up with sand brought down by the river Zwijn, till at the time when Karen lived, Bruges was no longer the proud and glorious city she had once been, but was all the while becoming poorer and poorer.

It was true there were many ancient families who still lived at ease in the beautiful old carved houses facing on shady squares or built along the edges of the winding canals that everywhere threaded the once busy city; though the quiet water of these now scarcely rippled save when the trailing branches of the overhanging willow trees dipped into them, or a fleet of stately white swans went sailing along. But in the poorer parts of the city the people must work hard, and there were whole streets where every one made lace; and all day long women and girls, old and young, bent over the black-covered pillows just as Karen's Grandmother was at that moment doing.

Grandmother's fingers steadily plied the tiny bobbins in and out long after Karen had put away her knitting and crept into the little cupboard bed which was built into the wall of the small room next to the living-room.

At last, as the candle burned low, the lace was finished; and carefully unpinning it from the pillow, Grandmother laid it in a clean napkin; and then she raked the ashes over the embers of the fire on the hearth, and soon her tired eyes closed in sleep as she lay in the high-posted bed close to Karen.

CHAPTER 2

BUYING THE PORRINGER

THE next morning was bright and clear, and the sun-
shine sparkled over the freshly fallen snow and touched all the
icicles with rainbow light.

Karen and her Grandmother were astir early. The little girl
fetched down some wood from the small attic, over the living-
room, where they kept their precious supply for the winter;
and then she set the table as Grandmother prepared the por-
ridge for their breakfast.

After breakfast Grandmother took her lace-pillow and began arranging her pins and bobbins for another piece of work;
and when Karen had dusted the simple furniture and swept the
snow from the doorstep, she put on her knitted hood and
shawl, and pinning together the napkin in which Grandmother
had placed the piece of lace, she set out for the home of Madame Koerner.

Down the narrow street she passed, and then across an old
stone bridge that spanned one of the lazy canals that wandered
through the city. The ice had spread a thin sheet over this, and
the beautiful white swans that swam about on it in the sum-
mer-time had gone into the shelter of their little wooden house,
which stood on the bank under a snowy willow tree. One of
the great shining birds, looking herself like a drift of snow,

stood at the door of the little shelter house preening her feathers in the sunlight, and Karen waved her hand to her with a smiling "Good-morning, Madame Swan!" for she loved the beautiful creatures, numbers of which are still seen on all the water-ways of Bruges, and she always spoke to them, and sometimes brought them crumbs from her bits of coarse bread at home.

Beyond the bridge she sped on past rows of tall brown houses with here and there a little shop crowded in between, and presently her way led across the Grande Place, a large, irregular square in the center of the city. Here there were many shops, and people passing to and fro; and among them went numbers of great shaggy dogs harnessed to little carts filled with vegetables or tall copper milk cans, and these they tugged across the cobblestones to the ancient Market Halles from which towered the wonderful belfry of which every one in Bruges was so proud.

Karen paused to listen while the silvery chimes rang out, as they had rung every quarter hour for more than three hundred years.

Then she passed on into a long, quiet street where the houses stood farther apart and had rows of trees in front of them. Some of them had high walls adjoining them, and behind these were pretty gardens, though now, of course, all were covered with the wintry snow.

Presently Karen stopped at a wooden gate leading into one of these gardens, and pushing it open made her way along a winding path to the door of a tall house with many gables and adorned with rare old carvings. This was the home of Madame Koerner; the house really faced on the street, but the little girl did not like to go to the more stately entrance, and so chose

[14]

the smaller one that opened into the garden. She knocked timidly, for she was a little in awe of Madame Koerner, who seemed to her a very grand lady. But the maid who opened the door knew Karen and led her in and took her at once to the upstairs room where Madame Koerner sat with a fine piece of needlework in her lap.

Madame Koerner smiled kindly at the little girl, who had several times before brought Grandmother's lace to her. "Good-morning, Karen," she said, "I am so glad to have the lace, for now I can finish this cap, which I want for a Christmas gift." And then as she unfolded the napkin and looked at the lace, "O," she cried, "how lovely it is! No one in all Bruges does more beautiful work than thy Grandmother, little one! And some day, I dare say, thou, too, wilt do just as well, for I know thou art learning fast." And she smiled again, and patted Karen's hands as the little girl held out the lace for her to see.

Karen colored with pleasure to hear Grandmother's work praised, as indeed it deserved; for the delicate scrolls and flowers and leaves of it looked as if made of frost and caught in a net of pearly cobwebs.

Madame Koerner was so pleased with it that when the little girl laid it down, she looked in her purse and gave her a generous gold piece for Grandmother, and then she added a smaller piece of silver for Karen herself; "That is for thee, little one," she said. "And I hope thou wilt have a very happy Christmas."

Karen thanked her shyly, and as with shining eyes she turned to go, Madame Koerner said, "Go out through the kitchen, child, and tell Marie, the cook, to fill thy napkin with some of the little cakes she is baking."

So when once more Karen tripped out into the street, her heart was very light and her mind full of happy thoughts as she tightly clasped in one hand the gold piece for Grandmother, and in the other the franc of silver which Madame Koerner had given for her own, and the napkin filled with the Christmas cakes. These were the kind that all Flemish children delight in, and were made of fine gingerbread and filled with candied orange peel and red cherries.

As Karen came near the Grande Place and saw the Market Halles, her eyes fairly danced, for she knew the Christmas market was going on there, and all the way from Madame Koerner's she had kept saying to herself: "Now I can buy a present for the Christ-child and one for Grandmother!"

Outside the Halles the cobblestones had been swept clean of snow, and a few hardy dealers had placed their wares for sale out of doors. But these were chiefly sellers of leather harnesses for the patient Flemish dogs, of wooden shoes and coarse baskets; and some had piled in front of them small bundles of fire-wood and fagots. But none of these wares interested Karen, and so she stepped inside the Halles where one might find all manner of things for sale. Here were stalls piled with different colored cloths, with kerchiefs and laces; in others were displayed great earthen pots and pans and other gear for the kitchen. And there were sellers of Christmas trinkets, and wax candles, and what not; of the milk in the tall copper cans the dogs had drawn thither in their little carts; of winter vegetables, and food and sweetmeats of various kinds.

"See!" called a white-capped woman, who sat behind a stall heaped with little cakes, "here are caraway cookies fit for the king's children, and only four sous the dozen!"

But Karen felt very rich with the Christmas cakes in her napkin, and so was not to be tempted. As she stepped slowly along, looking first at one side and then the other, presently she came to a stall where colored beads and trinkets of many kinds were arranged on a long strip of scarlet cloth. As she saw these, she could not help but stop and look longingly at a little necklace of blue beads, the very kind she had wanted for so long a time!

At this stall sat another whitecapped woman dealer, who, seeing the wistful look in Karen's face, said: "Well, my child, if thou canst give me ten sous, thou canst take home with thee this pretty trinket. 'Tis a fair match for thine eyes, little maid!"

Karen's blue eyes began to brim with tears, for she knew ten sous were only half a franc, and she did want the beads so very, very much! But after one more longing look she resolutely passed on, still tightly holding her silver franc; for, much as she wanted the necklace, she was determined that the Christ-child and Grandmother should have their gifts, and she was afraid even her wonderful franc might not be enough for all.

So she went on, still looking carefully at each stall she passed, and all the while growing more and more perplexed trying to decide which were the very prettiest things she could buy. She had gone more than half the length of the market, and was becoming bewildered and a little frightened as she hugged her shawl about her and made her way as best she could among the different groups of buyers and sellers. And then, by and by, her face lighted up with pleasure as she stopped in front of a pottery dealer's stall. This was presided over by a kindly faced man in a workman's blouse. On a smooth board in front of him were all kinds of the coarser wares of Flanders, and also some pieces made by the peasant folk of Normandy and Brittany, countries not far away; and among these smaller pieces Karen had spied a little porringer. It was just an humble little earthen dish such as the peasants of Brittany make for their children to use for their bread and milk; but it was gayly painted, and Karen thought it the most beautiful porringer she had ever seen. Its flat handles were colored a bright yet soft blue, and around the inner edge of its bowl were bands of blue and red, and right in the bottom was painted a little peasant girl; she wore a blue dress and a white and orange colored apron, and on her head was a pointed white cap. She carried in one hand a red rose, and on either side of her was a stiff little rose-tree with red blossoms. It was all crudely done, yet had a quaint charm of its own, a charm lacked by many a more finely finished piece; and it stood there leaning against a tall brown jar behind it, the little girl in the porringer seemed to smile back at Karen as she paused, rapt in admiration.

For Karen was quite sure that at last she had found the very thing for the blessed Christ-child. Indeed, she felt it was the one thing of all the things she had seen, that she most wanted to buy for him. And then, too, just beyond the porringer, a little farther down on the board, she saw a small, green jug that she was sure Grandmother would like. She wondered if they cost very much, and hardly dared to ask the pottery dealer. But presently she summoned up her courage, and, pointing to the little porringer and the jug, she said in a timid voice, "Please, sir, tell me, can I buy these for my franc?" And she held out to him her little palm, where lay the silver franc all warm and moist from the tight clasp of her rosy fingers.

The dealer looked at her anxious face and smiled at her as he said: "Dost thou want them so very much, little one? Truly thou canst have them for thy franc. My price would be some fifteen sous more, but for the sake of thy sweet face and the blessed Christmas time thou shalt have them." And he put them into Karen's arms as she smiled her delight.

The little girl was so happy that she fairly skimmed over the snowy cobblestones. When she came to the old bridge spanning the icy canal, the white swan was still standing on the bank blinking in the sunlight, and Karen called out merrily, "Dear Madame Swan, I have bought the most wonderful things!" And then she laughed a little silvery laugh, for her heart was so light it was fairly bubbling over with happiness.

When she reached the little yellow house she bounded up the step, and, standing on the sill close to the door, she called "Grandmother! Grandmother! Please let me in! I cannot open the door!"

Grandmother, hearing her, hurried to unlatch it, and Karen burst in with "Oh, Grandmother, see these beautiful Christmas cakes that Marie gave me! And here is a gold piece for your lace!"

And then having freed one hand, she pulled her shawl tightly together over the other things, and smiling delightedly, cried "And Madame Koerner gave me a silver franc for my very own, and I spent it in the Market Halles!"

"Thou hast already spent it?" asked Grandmother reprovingly. "Karen! Karen! wilt thou never learn to save thy pennies? What hast thou bought?"

"Oh," answered Karen, as her face fell, "I wanted one of them to be a secret till to-morrow! They are Christmas presents! But I wanted to show the other"—here she broke off confusedly; she had meant to say she wanted to show the porringer to Grandmother, but now she had not the heart. "But, Grandmother," she went on earnestly, "it was my own franc, and I love to buy gifts! And you know I couldn't last year because I had no pennies."

"Well, well, child," said Grandmother softening, "thou hast a generous heart, only thou shouldst not have spent all thy franc; thou hadst done better to put some by for another time."

Karen said nothing, though the tears of disappointment sprang to her eyes. She had wanted so much to show the porringer and share her joy in it with Grandmother. But now she felt that it would not be approved of since Grandmother thought her so foolish to spend all her franc, and especially since she had said that no one gave Christmas presents to the Christ-child. But though that had seemed to settle the matter for Grandmother, it only made Karen the more anxious to do so. She said to herself that if no one gave the Christ-child presents, it was all the more reason why she should—surely somebody ought to! And so she was not in the least sorry that she had not saved any of her franc. And she tried to think, too, that perhaps Grandmother would like a Christmas present herself, for all she said the money should not have been spent; perhaps when Grandmother saw the little green jug, she would think it so pretty that she would be glad that Karen had bought it. But she was not to see it till Christmas morning, for Karen meant to put it in her shoe just as the Christ-child did for children.

So presently her face brightening up, while Grandmother went on with her work, she ran into the other room and pulling open a deep drawer from a clothes-press that stood against the wall, she thrust the precious gifts under the folded clothes to stay hidden until she wanted them.

After dinner Grandmother began to prick the pattern for the new piece of lace she was beginning, and Karen knitted a while until it was time for the vesper service in the old cathedral of Saint Sauveur, whose tall tower rose above the steep housetops not far away.

When the bells began chiming, Grandmother and the little girl, laying aside their work, made themselves ready; and each carrying a white wax candle, which Grandmother had taken pains to provide some time before, they trudged off down the street.

When they reached the cathedral and entered through the great carved portal, the late afternoon light was falling in softly colored bars through the multitude of richly stained windows. As Karen gazed around at the many shrines where hundreds of wax tapers brought by other worshippers were already dotting the brightly colored air with their tiny golden flames, they looked so beautiful that for a moment she wondered if perhaps after all the Christ-child might not like the wax candles best. But the more she thought, she decided that he would surely be pleased to have something for really his own; for, of course, the candles were partly for God and the Blessed Virgin; and so she was glad she had the porringer that should be entirely his.

After the vesper service was over, and they were back again in the little house, the rest of the day passed very quickly for Karen. After supper Grandmother dozed a while in her chair beside the hearth; and then Karen ran into their sleeping-room and hurriedly took out the porringer and the green jug from their hiding-place in the clothes-press. Grandmother had put on some old slippers in place of the heavy wooden shoes she had worn all day, and these sabots were standing on the floor near her bed.

The room was dark, but Karen felt around till she found the sabots; and then she gave a little suppressed laugh of pleasure as she thrust the little green jug as far as it would go in one of them. She knew Grandmother would not find it till morning, for they never thought of having a light by which to go to bed; a candle for the living-room was all they could afford.

After placing the green jug in Grandmother's shoe, Karen stood for a moment thinking where she would put the porringer. She wanted the Christ-child to find it without any trouble; for he must be in a great hurry with so many children's houses to visit and sabots to fill. She thought first that when she took off hers for the night and stood them on the hearth to wait for him, she would set the porringer beside them. But then she remembered that at midnight, when he would come, the room would be quite dark; for Grandmother would put out the candle, and cover up the fire with ashes. And while, of course, the Christ-child expected sabots to be ready for him on the hearth and so could fill them in the dark, just as she had put the jug in Grandmother's, still, he might miss the porringer as that he would not be expecting, and so would not look for it.

Then, all at once, Karen remembered that out of doors it was moonlight; for, when she had fastened the wooden shutters at the front windows, the moon was rising round and silvery above the peaked roofs across the way. As she thought of this her perplexity vanished, and again a smile came to her lips as she said to herself: "I will set it outside on the doorstep, and the Christ-child will be sure to see it when he comes, and, of course, he will know it was meant for him, for he knows all about Christmas presents!"

Karen was greatly pleased with this plan; and so giving one more look at the little girl in the porringer, she took up two of the Christmas cakes from the dish on the table, and, squeezing them into its bowl, she went to the door and softly unbarred it; then, setting the porringer on the doorstep where the moonlight touched it, she again shut and fastened the door.

Grandmother roused from her doze before long, and sent Karen to bed, while she herself stayed up to knit to the end of her skein.

But long after the little girl lay in her cupboard bed her blue eyes were wide open with excitement. On the hearth in the living-room stood her little wooden shoes waiting for the visit of the Christ-child, and she longed with all her might to see him! And she longed, too, to know if he would be pleased with the porringer. But Grandmother had always told her that he did not like to be watched, and would not come till children were asleep.

By and by, after what seemed to Karen a very long time, her eyes began to blink, and she fell asleep and slept so soundly that she did not know when Grandmother put out the candle and covered up the fire and came to bed. Nor did she waken later on when peals of bells from the tall belfry and the cathedral and all the many churches of Bruges rang in the Christmas, and the sweet echoes of chanting voices and the songs of innumerable choristers floated over the city as the holy midnight mass was celebrated.

The rain of music thrilled and quivered through the frosty air, and then slowly it died away; and the Christmas stars shone and twinkled, and the great silver moon flooded the quiet night with a white radiance.

CHAPTER 3

ROBBER HANS

THE midnight music had ceased for some time, and

The Little Street Of The Holy Ghost was very quiet and deserted, as indeed it had been all the evening. But presently any one looking up it might have seen a man moving swiftly along. He did not walk like honest folk, but trod softly on the narrow flagstones close to the tall old houses, and seemed to try to keep within their shadows; and his eyes were all the while alertly watching everything about him.

As he came in front of the little yellow house the moon was slowly sinking behind a high gable across the street, but a last ray of silvery light fell across the doorstep, and just touched the edge of the porringer as it stood where Karen had placed it.

The man's keen eyes caught the gleam of something there, and though he could not tell exactly what it was, as the moonlight was waning fast, he nevertheless stooped quickly, and seizing the porringer in his hand, thrust it into the great pocket of his ragged coat. Then he hurried on and turned the corner and soon was lost in the shadows of a narrow passageway between two old houses.

Now, this man was known among evil-doers as "Hans the Robber," and many times the watchmen of Bruges had tried to catch him and punish him because he had stolen so many things from honest folk.

But always he managed to get away from them; or, if they came to the miserable hut where he lived at the edge of the city, he had some story to tell that deceived them so they could prove nothing against him, or else he contrived to hide until they got tired searching for him.

But people suspected him and shunned him as much as possible. On this night he had gone out hoping that while many were in the churches attending the midnight mass, he might find a chance to creep into some house and rob the owner of whatever he could. But he had not had good success in his dishonest work. To be sure, he had stolen a silver cup from one place; but then he had been frightened off before he could secure more, and so he had decided to try another and quieter part of the city; and as he came along the deserted Little Street Of The Holy Ghost and saw the porringer on the doorstep, he took it, because he always took everything he could.

When, after dropping it into his pocket, he went around the corner and into the passage-way, he reached his hand stealthily through the half closed shutters of a tall house beside him and tried to unfasten the window so that he might steal in. But just then he heard some one stirring within, and angrily muttering to himself, he fled away.

Here and there, as he hurried along, the waning moonbeams still shed a lingering light; and besides, it was getting so near dawn time that at last he decided that it was no use trying to get in anywhere else that night; and so he went back to his hut. When he reached this, he first carefully hid the silver cup he had stolen, by putting it in a cranny under a loose

[26]

board in the floor; then throwing himself down on a rude bed of straw heaped in a corner, he soon fell into a heavy sleep.

When Hans the Robber awoke next morning, the hut was cold and cheerless. He rose from his wretched bed, and found a few billets of wood with which he kindled some fire on the untidy hearth.

In the bare cupboard he found little save crusts of black bread; and as he ate these he sat down on a rickety bench, which he pulled close to the fire, and drew his ragged coat closer around him.

Everything looked very dreary and desolate to him; and, as he heard the Christmas bells beginning to ring, a bitter look came into his face, for it had been many years since Christmas had meant anything to Robber Hans. He shrugged his shoulders, and thrust both hands into the pockets of his coat. As he did so, he felt something in one of them which he had forgotten all about; and then drawing out the little porringer, which still held the two Christmas cakes, he stared at it in surprise.

"Now, where could I have picked up that?" he said to himself, as he set it down on the bench beside him. Then he remembered how he had taken some object from the doorstep of a little yellow house that stood on a corner.

He took up one of the little cakes and broke it, and, as he was hungry, in two bites he had eaten it. As he took the other one in his fingers, he began to look at it curiously and to think.

Robber Hans had not eaten a little cake like that for years and years. All at once, with a start, old memories began to waken in his mind; for the little cake made him think of when he was a little boy and his mother had made just such wonderful little ginger cakes full of orange-peel and red cherries. And then, as he looked at the empty porringer, he stared at it with an almost startled look, for he remembered how he used to eat his bread and milk from a porringer exactly like that; only instead of a little girl painted in the bowl, in his was a little boy. Robber Hans could remember precisely how that little boy looked in his blue blouse and wooden shoes, and on his head a broad-brimmed hat of Breton straw, with a red ribbon on it.

For Robber Hans as a child had lived in the old seaport town of Quiberon, in Brittany, where his father was a fisherman. His mother's home before she married had been in Bruges, and so it was that at holiday time she always made for the little family of children the Christmas cakes like that which Robber Hans now held in his hand.

As he remembered all these things he forgot all about being cold and hungry. Presently, laying down the little cake, he took up the porringer and looked closely at the little girl holding the red rose in her hand.

Robber Hans in those far-away days had had a little sister whom he dearly loved; and the more he looked at the little girl in the porringer, the more he thought of his little sister Emschen, till presently he was sure that the face looking up at him from under the stiff white cap was the face of Emschen. It did not matter whether it looked like the little sister or not, for before the eyes of Robber Hans memory was bringing back her face so clearly that to him it seemed really there. Yes, and he was quite sure, too, that Emschen had worn a little apron like that; and there was the rose in her hand, and he remembered how she had loved roses!

It all came back to him how when they were children together he had made a little flower bed for her, close by their cottage door, and how both of them had carried white scallop shells from the edge of the sea and laid them around it, making a pretty border; and how pleased Emschen had been when her first little rosebush had a blossom, and how wonderfully it had flourished in the salt sea air, as do all the roses of Brittany.

And then more and more things came back to his memory, and the longer he looked and thought, his own face began gradually to soften, till, by and by, the oddest thing happened—a great tear fell into the porringer and lay there like a drop of dew on one of the painted rose-trees!

At this he roused himself, and, quickly brushing his hand across his eyes, he angrily thrust the porringer from him, and the bitter look came back into his face. For his memory, having started, would not stop with the pleasant days when he was a little boy in Quiberon, but went on and on, bringing freshly back to him how father, mother, and Emschen, all were gone; the father drowned in the stormy Breton sea, and the mother and Emschen sleeping in the wind-swept God's acre of Quiberon, with no one to lay on their graves even so much as a green holly leaf at Christmas time, or a wild poppy flower on Midsummer day. He saw in memory his brothers grown up and scattered from the old home, and himself become a sailor roving the sea to many lands; and then later on drifting ashore in the Flemish country, and overtaken by misfortune after misfortune, till at last he had fallen so low that here in Bruges, his mother's old home, he was known only as Robber Hans!

He rose to his feet, and, in a fit of sudden anger, because of his wasted and unhappy life, he seized the little porringer which had reminded him of what he had lost, and was about to dash it to pieces on the bricks of the hearth. But, just as he raised his hand, something seemed to stop him. He could not tell why, but instead of breaking the porringer he slowly walked over to the empty cupboard and placed it on the shelf. Then, bewildered by his own action, he stood a moment and stared at it.

Presently, as his unhappy thoughts came crowding back again, his bitterness and anger rose as before, and he wanted to be rid of the porringer. But instead of trying to break it this time, another idea occurred to him. "There!" he muttered gruffly to himself, as he turned away from the cupboard, "It can stay there till to-morrow, and then I will take it with the silver cup and sell it at the thieves' market!"

That was a place in the old city where those who lived by stealing from others were accustomed to dispose of their spoils; and so among themselves they called it the "thieves' market." The dealer who kept the place and who bought their stolen articles knew how to send them around quietly and sell them, usually in other cities, where there was less danger of their being discovered by their rightful owners.

Robber Hans had many times before disposed of his dishonestly gotten things to the keeper of the thieves' market; and so when he made up his mind to sell the porringer along with the silver cup, he knew very well where to take them. But he knew, too, that he would have to wait till the next day, for the dealer would probably not be in his place until Christmas was over.

Having thus made up his mind how to rid himself of the porringer, and meantime having nothing to do in the hut, he thrust on his battered cap, and pulling it down over his eyes, he strode out into the street.

After wandering aimlessly about for some time, at last he made his way to a certain quay, or open space, on the edge of one of the many old canals of the city. There were numbers of these embankments which had been made, in the days of Bruges' prosperity, as mooring places for the freighted barges that carried her commerce. And though the barges had long since deserted all but a few of the quiet waterways, still the quays bore their old Flemish names. Thus, the one to which Hans had wandered was called the Quai du Rosaire. Here a moss-grown stone bridge crossed the water, and in a paved square near by and in a tumbledown old brown house facing the square, for three days of every week a fish market was held. And here, on holidays, the rougher folk of Bruges would gather to amuse themselves.

Robber Hans crossed the paved square and entered the old house, where he was greeted boisterously as he joined the noisy company. But somehow their rough talk and rude actions did not please him as they had often done before. He was silent and moody, and at last the others taunted him so with his sour looks, that he got up from a bench where he was sitting beside a tipsy fishmonger, and, flinging back some scornful words, he left the place and went out.

Again he wandered aimlessly along the snowy streets; till after a while the wintry wind blew through his ragged coat and he shivered with cold. He was, by this time, near the great square where the belfry rose from the Halles, and making his way to this, he crept into the shelter of its entrance. Then, in a little while, he ventured inside and dropped down on the long, wooden seat between its tall windows. And though many who came and went through the Halles looked at him suspiciously, no one cared to make him go away, for it was the blessed

Christmas day, and so the hearts of all were kindlier for the while.

As he leaned back against the wall, by and by the warmth of the room made him drowsy and he fell asleep. And, as he slept, there flitted through his brain a great many confused dreams; and with almost all of them the thoughts started by the little porringer seemed somehow to be connected. Sometimes he dreamed he was a little boy again, in Quiberon; and then Emschen would seem to be running toward him with a red rose in her hand; but always when she came near to him, though she put out her hands to him, he could not touch her, and the red rose faded and fell apart. And then the dreams trailed off so dim and shadowy that when at last he awakened Hans could not remember just what it was that he had been dreaming. He only vaguely knew that it had something to do with the porringer and that it had made him unhappy; and as he stumbled to his feet and set out for his hut, he again determined to get rid of it as soon as he could.

CHAPTER 4

ROBBER HANS AND THE PORRINGER

THE next morning Hans thrust in his pocket the silver cup and the porringer, which he took pains not to look at again, and went out to find the dealer to whom he might sell them.

He threaded his way through the narrow, crooked streets till by and by he came to a rickety wooden house standing behind some tall old warehouses that fronted on a canal. These had once been piled high with rich stuffs in the great days of Bruges, but now they were deserted and falling into decay.

Hans, after looking cautiously about him, quickly approached the rickety house and knocked in an odd way, which was his signal, so that the dealer within would know it was not one of the officers of the city come to arrest him. For, of course, it was against the law to buy stolen goods; though the laws then in Bruges were not so well looked after as they should have been. And so the dishonest trade within the old house had been carried on for some time undisturbed.

As Hans now entered the heavy wooden door, which he quickly closed and barred behind him, he found himself in a dimly lighted room where the brown rafters showed hung thick with cobwebs. This was the place known to him and his kind as the "thieves' market." Around the walls were a number of shelves and on these were arranged all manner of things; some of them costly and others of little value, but all stolen from one place or another; for this was a favorite spot for evil-doers to dispose of their plunder.

As Hans strode to the middle of the room and stood before a narrow counter that divided it, a little old man, who was busy sorting some wares behind a pile of boxes, turned around with "Good day, Robber Hans! And what hast thou brought to Father Deaf-and-Blind?" For so the little old man, with his cunning eyes and hard, wicked face, was called by those who dealt with him; because he always pretended that he neither saw nor heard that the things they brought to sell had been stolen from their rightful owners.

But Hans was in no mood for talk as sullenly he drew from his pocket the silver cup and without a word placed it on the counter.

"Ah!" cried the little old man, greedily seizing the cup and looking closely at it. "This mark must come off; yes, and this coat-of-arms! Hm, 'twill be some trouble to do that skillfully!" And then turning it round again and considering the coat-of-arms, "Let me see," he went on inquiringly, still looking at it. "There! now I have it! 'Tis the mark of the Groene family. Have they 'presented' this to thee lately, or is it one of the 'gifts' of last month, when several families were so generous to thee, eh?"

This pretending that they were presents was the usual way in which Father Deaf-and-Blind asked about stolen goods; and as now he chuckled and fixed his shrewd eyes upon Hans, the latter muttered a low reply, and, after some chaffering, the old man took a bag from an iron box under the counter and counted out a sum of silver, which Hans swept into his pocket. Then he took out the porringer and set it beside the cup.

"Ho," said the old man contemptuously, "I'll warrant such peasant gear was never sheltered under the same roof as this silver cup!" For in the stately old homes of Bruges, such as that of the Groene family, where things had been handed down from generation to generation, even the pots and pans in the kitchens were of fine and costly workmanship. And the moment he looked at it, Father Deaf-and-Blind knew very well that the little earthenware porringer had been made by peasant folk for the use of humble people like themselves.

And so the old dealer, giving it another brief glance, added: "Thou must have picked up that while paying a visit to the children's God's-House!" For so the people of Bruges called the almshouse where the homeless children of the poor were sheltered and cared for.

Hans had turned away his eyes when he set the porringer down, for he did not want to see it again and have the old memories come back to haunt him. But now, before he knew what he was doing, he looked down in the bowl, straight into the face of the little girl; and immediately it became the face of Emschen, and her eyes looked up so mournfully into the eyes of Robber Hans, and the little smile on her lips was so sad it was as if her heart was breaking! And Hans, turning very white, scarcely knew what he did as he put out his hand tremblingly and carefully lifted the porringer from the counter.

"Hold!" cried Father Deaf-and-Blind, who was surprised at Hans' action, and who really thought the porringer a quaint and pretty bit of earthenware, " 'tis not so bad for some burgher customer. I will give five sous for it."

But Hans had already replaced the porringer in his pocket, and without another word he turned, and going straight to the door, he unbarred it and went out.

As the old man swiftly crossed the room to refasten the door, he muttered to himself, "I wonder what ails friend Hans this morning? He is as cross as a fishwife when the catch is bad, and he acts as if he had been robbed of his wits or else left them behind in his miserable hut!" And then he went back to the counter and began to weigh the silver cup and consider how he could best smooth away the tell-tale marks.

As for Robber Hans, when again he found himself walking the snowy streets, he walked as one in a dream. It was no use trying to avoid it; the sad little face of Emschen seemed to hover before his eyes wherever he turned; and another thing, of which he had not before thought, began to trouble him. Old Father Deaf-and-Blind's chance speech about the children's God's-House had reminded him that the porringer he had stolen must have belonged to some poor child and, for the first time in a great many years, Hans really began to feel ashamed of himself. He tried again to remember just where he had picked up the porringer; and though it had not occurred to him at the time he took it, now he said to himself: "Why was it outside on the doorstep? 'Twas a queer place to find it!"

Hans wished with all his heart that he had let it stay there, since it was making him so uncomfortable and seemed so impossible to get rid of, or even to get it out of his thoughts! For still his mind went on puzzling to account for the porringer having been on the doorstep. Finally, however, he decided that as it was on the night before Christmas that he had taken it, probably it was a gift that some friend had brought for a child who must live in the little yellow house; and perhaps no one had been at home to open the door, and so the porringer had been left on the step.

Having explained it to himself in this way, for the first time such an idea had troubled him since he had become a robber, the feeling came to him that he ought to take it back where it belonged—it seemed so shameful to rob a child, and a poor child at that! But, he thought, he could not take it back in broad daylight! No, he decided, if he did so, it must be after night, when no one could see him.

As he was thinking all this over, without noticing where he was going, his steps had brought him to the part of the city where there were a number of shops, and he remembered that he was hungry, for he had had no breakfast. He went into one of the shops and asked for some food. The shopkeeper looked at him suspiciously. "Thou art a burly beggar!" he said. "There are far too many needy poor in Bruges to give to such as thou!"

"I am no beggar!" said Hans, angrily, displaying one of his silver coins. "Here is silver for thy meat and bread, and see to it thou dost not cheat me!"

The shopkeeper, muttering to himself, supplied a dish of food; though he was glad when Hans had finished eating it and left the shop, for he did not think that he looked like an honest man or that he had come by the silver honestly. Now, on Hans' part, when in order to pay the shopkeeper he had put his hand in his pocket for a piece of the silver he had received for the stolen cup, his fingers touched the porringer first; and, he could not have told why, he took the rest of the silver out and put it in the pocket on the other side of his coat.

Perhaps, in some vague way, he did not quite like to have that ill-gotten money right there with the picture of Emschen;

[37]

for to his mind the little girl in the porringer had become so bound up with Emschen that it might as well have really been her picture.

And then as Hans went farther along the street, he did another queer thing; he deliberately turned down a narrow way that led to one of the many old quays of the city, and began to look at the ships that were lying moored close beside it.

In the days of the bygone glory of Bruges, her harbor, now choked up with sand, and her many canals, had been thronged with vessels from all over the world, and every quay had been a place of busy work all day long and often through the night. And now, though most of them were deserted and moss-grown, still on the banks of one canal, which connected Bruges with the not far distant sea-port city of Ostend, there were several quays to which came small fishing vessels and various ships that traded along the coast of Flanders.

It happened that on that day there were two or three schooners lying at the quay to which Hans had come. He had come there because with all the thoughts of his childhood that had been stirred to life by the little porringer, there had wakened the memory of the sea as it rolled and surged beyond the grey rocks of the Quiberon coast. He began to long for the familiar tang of the fresh salt air blowing over the curling green waves, and to sail over these as he had once done in the old days when he had first set out to make his way in the world. For, like most of the folk of the Breton coast, Hans seemed to belong to the sea. And he had been a good sailor in those days. But though he had drifted away from that old life and his old friends, and had for so long a while gained his living by robbery that all thought of the past seemed dead within him, as he now looked at the vessels rocking on the water by the quay, stronger and stronger grew his newly awakened longing for the sea, till at last it swept over him like a fierce gust of the north wind that he had often seen dashing the white-capped waves against the crags of Quiberon.

And along with this great longing, all the while stronger and stronger grew another wish; though, curiously enough, Hans himself could not for the life of him have told that he had it. It was a wish to lead an honest life once more; it had really always been down in the bottom of his heart, but it had gotten so covered up and hidden by all sorts of robber thoughts that now it was like a ray of light trying to shine through a window all covered with dust and cobwebs. And so all Hans knew about it was that he wanted more than anything else to be a sailor on one of those vessels.

Hans walked along the quay till he came alongside the nearest of the schooners he had been watching, and then he hailed the captain, who was standing on the deck.

"What do you want?" asked the captain, looking at Hans, and not with favor.

"Do you need another hand on your boat?" asked Hans.

"No," answered the captain shortly, and turned away contemptuously without paying any further attention.

Hans' temper began to rise as he strode along toward where the next vessel lay. Two of her crew were unloading her cargo under the direction of the captain. After looking at them a moment, "Ho!" called Hans abruptly to the men, "you handle that gear like the veriest landlubbers! Give me a chance, and I'll show you how to unload yonder bales in a quarter the time it is taking you!"

Of course this was a very poor way to go about it if he wanted to get work on that boat; but Hans had little tact at best, and moreover he had been stung by the manner of the captain of the other vessel, and so his ill humor had gotten the better of him.

At his speech, the two men looked up in surprise, and seeing Hans' ragged figure, one of them, who knew him by sight, cried out jeeringly, "Hold thy tongue, thou impudent beggar! I'll warrant thou couldst lighten one of these bales in a twinkling couldst thou but get thy thieving fingers upon it! Begone!"

Hans' eyes blazed, and he strode forward with fist clenched to strike the man. But the latter was too nimble; for the two, having finished their work, ran up the gang-plank and drew it in, so that Hans could not reach them, and they laughed scornfully as they taunted him from their place on the deck.

Hans was very angry and his heart full of bitterness. He turned on his heel and half started away from the quay. But, like many other people of strong will, to be crossed in what he wished to do only made Hans more unwilling to give it up. And so the harder it seemed to be to get a place on one of those vessels the more he wanted it. And turning back again, he determined to try once more.

This time he went to the far end of the quay, where a fishing vessel was moored. The captain was standing on the bank near the side of the boat, and Hans, walking up to him, said: "I am going to ship as sailor on this vessel."

Captain Helmgar, for this was his name, gave a short laugh as he looked at the man in front of him. "Ho," he said, "not so fast, my man! I am owner of this craft, and I choose my own crew! I'll wager thou dost not know the tiller from the forecastle!"

"Just try me!" cried Hans eagerly. "Your craft is in fair order, but yonder sail was shrouded by a bungling hand!" and Hans pointed to one of the masts of the vessel, where the sail was furled in a way that his practiced eye at once saw was clumsy.

At this the captain opened his eyes and stared at Hans; for it was perfectly true that one of the crew was a lazy, ignorant fellow who had no fondness for the sea and who bungled everything he touched, and Captain Helmgar was really anxious to replace him with an experienced sailor. As he now began to question Hans, he soon discovered that he knew all about ships and shipping, as did almost all the men brought up on the coast of Brittany; and then, too, Hans' experience as sailor had been chiefly on fishing vessels.

The captain did not like Hans' raggedness and unkempt looks, and, though he knew nothing about him, was rather suspicious of his honesty. But then he needed a man, and Hans certainly seemed to know his trade. Captain Helmgar, moreover, was a good-hearted man, and thought to himself, "There is little on a fishing vessel he could steal, even if he is a thief." The captain, too, rather liked Hans' determination to ship with him; so after thinking a few minutes, he said "Well, my man, we leave for a week's cruise to-morrow morning at eight o'clock, and, if you report on time, I will take you on trial."

CHAPTER 5

HANS TURNS SAILOR

As Hans turned away from the quay his heart was lighter than it had been for many a day. He straightened up, and no longer sought all the narrower by-ways as he had long grown used to doing; but beginning to feel already like an honest man, he walked boldly down the chief streets of the city. And though now and then people glanced at him and drew away from him, he looked straight ahead, his mind busy with plans for the future.

He crossed the Grande Place, and presently, as he passed the doorway of the cathedral of Saint Sauveur, he saw an old woman crouching against the wall and begging for alms. With a sudden impulse he thrust his hand into the pocket where lay the silver pieces Father Deaf-and-Blind had paid for the stolen cup, and drawing them out he dropped them into the old woman's lap, and hastened on before she could speak for amazement.

When he got back to his hut it was almost dusk. He made a fire with the last bit of wood, and ate the last crusts of bread he could find in the cupboard; and then, filled with thoughts of the next day, and saying over to himself with a sort of pleased surprise, "I am really going to be a sailor again! I am going to the sea!" he went to sleep and slept soundly until daybreak.

As soon as Hans awakened he remembered what he was to do, and so he made himself as tidy as he could; which was not much, to be sure, but still he looked a little less unkempt than usual. Just before he started out, he happened to put his hand in his pocket and there was still the porringer! He quickly drew away his fingers from it as if it burned them—but then again he put back his hand and took out the little dish.

He scowled a little as he looked at the troublesome porringer and remembered that after he had left old Father Deaf-and-Blind the morning before, he had meant to take it back as soon as dark fell and leave it on the doorstep where he had found it. He was annoyed that his mind had been so full of his new plans that he had forgotten all about it when night came, and now he knew he would not have time to hunt up the little yellow house, even if he wanted to restore the porringer by daylight and run the risk of having to make explanation of his act.

So holding it a moment uncertainly, presently he walked over to the empty cupboard and stood it up at the back of the shelf. He thought that when he came back at the end of the week, he would see about taking it to the little house. Then he pulled the door shut behind him, and leaving the hut set out for the quay.

At the end of a week the fishing vessel was again moored in the old canal of Bruges. The catch had been good, and there was a great chattering among the fish-wives who came to buy the fish as they were unloaded from the vessel. By and by, a group of them caught sight of Hans, who was busily helping carry the cargo to shore.

"Look!" they cried, pointing their fingers at him, "There is Hans the Robber! We have missed him for a whole week! So he has turned sailor again! Ho! Ho! Hans, Hans! Didst thou rob the captain of that coat?"

"No!" said Captain Helmgar, who was close by and listening sharply to their wagging tongues, "No! Hush your clamor! I gave him the coat myself, and he is the best sailor that ever trod yonder deck!" and he waved his hand toward the vessel beside him.

Now, Captain Helmgar quickly understood from the fish-wives' talk that Hans had indeed borne a bad name, as he had suspected the day he had first talked with him. But, nevertheless, he determined to give him a fair chance to earn an honest living. In the week Hans had been on the vessel he had proven a fine sailor and had worked hard and faithfully; and Captain Helmgar thought it a shame not to help him if he was really trying to do better. So, when he paid him his wages for the week's work, he shook him heartily by the hand and told him that he had done well, and that the next day they would set out again and that he would expect Hans to go with them. "And you might as well live on the boat while you work for me," added Captain Helmgar kindly, "for perhaps you have no home of your own."

"No," said Hans, "I have none; nothing but an old tumble-down hut that I would be glad never to see again!" But just then he remembered the porringer, which had quite passed out of his mind in the busy week of the new life he had begun. He felt that he must get it if it was still where he had left it; for though he considered that the little dish had caused him no end of bother, he had not given up the idea of taking it back where it belonged.

So turning again to Captain Helmgar, he said, "It is only a miserable place, the old hut, but there is something there I must get before I come to stay on the boat."

"Very well," replied the captain, "go and get whatever you want; but be sure and be back by afternoon, for there will be plenty of work here to get ready for sailing to-morrow."

As Hans started off down the street he decided that this was as good a time as any to hunt for the little yellow house; for if he could slip away from the fishing vessel for a little while that evening, as he hoped, he wanted to know exactly where the house stood so he need waste no time finding it.

So he threaded his way through the maze of cobble-paved streets as nearly as he could remember in the direction he had gone on the night before Christmas. At last he turned into The Little Street Of The Holy Ghost, and, looking down it, yes, he was certain this was the one for which he was searching.

Slackening his steps, as he walked slowly along he kept looking out for the little house, which he had passed hurriedly that Christmas eve and without especially noticing it; though he remembered that it stood on a corner, and he felt sure he would know it again.

Before long he came to it, and, sure enough, he knew it at once. There was the wooden step on which the porringer had stood, and Karen, with her little shawl pinned about her shoulders, was sweeping it. As Hans walked slowly by, suddenly he stopped and said to Karen, "What is thy name, little girl?"

Karen timidly lifted her blue eyes to his, and "Karen, sir," she answered simply.

"Hast thou any brothers or sisters?" continued Hans.

"No, sir," said Karen wonderingly, "there is no one but Grandmother and me. Did you want to see Grandmother?"

"No, no," muttered Hans hastily; and then, feeling that he must make some excuse for his questions, "I was only hunting where some one lives," he added, and with an awkward bow to the little girl he passed hurriedly on; though in doing so his keen eyes had noticed Grandmother at the window bending over her lace-pillow.

"So," he said to himself, "that is the child the porringer belongs to; and her Grandmother is a lace-maker!" And again shame came to him because he had taken the gift he felt sure had been meant for the little blue-eyed girl.

He went on to the old tumbledown hut and pushed open the door. No one had disturbed the place since he had left it; indeed, it had been deserted when Hans had taken possession of it, and since then no one had dared molest it. The hut looked very bare and forlorn as Hans stepped into it, and there was really nothing in it that he cared to take with him; that is, nothing but the little porringer, which still stood back in the dusty corner of the old cupboard. As he lifted it down and looked at it, he fancied that Emschen smiled up at him happily from between the rose-trees of the bowl; and he tucked it very carefully into the pocket of the decent coat Captain Helmgar had given him.

"Then he went back, retracing his steps all the way till he reached The Little Street Of The Holy Ghost. When again he came to the yellow house the door was closed; and he had half a notion that he would hurriedly set the porringer down on the step, even if it was daylight.

But as he glanced up at the two little windows, there were Grandmother and Karen, and he could not do it right under their eyes!

Hans frowned; it seemed as if he never could get rid of this last bit of stolen property. For though he really wanted to give the porringer back to Karen, he could not bring himself to take it to her and tell her he had stolen it; nor could he bear to have her see him leave it on the step and guess that he had been a thief.

So there seemed nothing left for him to do but to carry it on to the fishing vessel and put it in the locker where he kept his few clothes, and then wait for evening or some other chance to restore it. But the chance did not come that evening, for Captain Helmgar had many things for the sailors to do on the vessel, and so Hans had to put off taking home the porringer till some other time when he would return to Bruges.

And the odd part about it all was that the longer Hans had the little porringer near him, the more attached to it he grew, and the more he came to hate the thought of giving it up! He kept it in his locker, and every day he looked at it until he became almost superstitious about it. Sometimes the little girl in it made him think of Karen, but more often it was Emschen, and always when he tried hard to do well he thought the face smiled at him but when sometimes at first the work seemed hard and he would half think of going back to his old robber life, then the little girl in the porringer looked so sad and mournful that Hans always gave over those half formed ideas and kept honestly on, doing his work so well that Captain Helmgar came more and more to trust and depend upon him.

CHAPTER 6

AT THE RAG-MARKET

WHILE the fishing vessel was going up and down the Flemish coast, and every little while coming back to the quay at Bruges, the winter was wearing away, and along the water-courses and open squares of the city the chestnut and willow trees were putting on their April greenery.

Crocuses and hyacinths were blooming in many little nooks by the lazy canals where the white swans and ducks sailed happily, guiding their downy flocks of young. Sweeping the placid mirror of the Minne-Water out by the ancient city gateway, the stately elms were hung with pale green tassels, and, hidden among these, nightingales fluted all night long. While in the gardens by the tall brown houses in the older parts of the city, cuckoos and starlings sang all day from blossoming apple and cherry boughs.

Though on The Little Street Of The Holy Ghost the dwellings stood close to the cobblestones, and so had no dooryards for grass or flowers, nevertheless through the open windows of the little yellow house the spring wind blew in softly, laden with April fragrance. But by the window in the living-room Grandmother could not be seen bending over her lace-making as for so many years before. Instead, she lay propped up in her bed, too ill and weak to guide the bobbins full of delicate thread that hung idly from the pillow near by.

Poor Grandmother had been unable to work for several weeks; and, though better of her illness, strength came back but slowly to her trembling hands. Karen had had a sad and sorry time, too; for she was only a little girl, and every day there was so much work to do. Their neighbor folk had been good and kind, and had done all they could to help take care of Grandmother; but the little savings she had laid away were almost gone, and her great fear now was that she would be forced to go to one of the God's Houses; for besides those for children, there were many other almshouses in Bruges that bore this name. There were many of these because poverty lay heavily on the poorer people, and if they fell ill it meant bitter suffering.

Grandmother wished passionately to be able to stay in the little home where she had always lived, and to keep Karen with her.

So long as she could work at her lace-pillow she could manage this; but now her hands were idle, and Karen too young and her little fingers as yet untrained save for the simplest stitches; and so the pinch of want had come upon them, and with all Grandmother's pride it seemed no longer possible to live unless help came in some way.

Madame Koerner would no doubt have befriended them had she known their need. But Madame Koerner was not then in Bruges. She had been called to the city of Ghent by the illness of her own mother, and, in her anxiety for her, she did not know of the sore straits to which Grandmother and Karen had come.

As Grandmother now lay in her bed, she was thinking hard of how they might get a little money to keep them in food until she could gain enough strength to work again.

Presently, "Karen!" she called to the little girl who was in the living-room bending over her lace-pillow and trying hard to make some of the stitches she had been taught last. But the thread was so fine and it was so hard to manage the bobbins exactly right that her forehead was all puckered and the tears lay very near her eyes.

"Yes, Grandmother," she answered, as she laid down the bobbins, and jumping up from her stool went and stood by the bedside.

"Karen," said Grandmother, in a weak voice, "I have been thinking that to-day is the day for the rag-market down by the Quai Vert, and neighbor Radenour told me yesterday that she had some extra cloth from her weaving and she means to take it there to sell. And, Karen,"—Grandmother's voice was very low and sad, but she went bravely on,—"canst not thou go with her and take the two brass candlesticks? It may be thou canst sell them for a fair price, and we are sorely in need of money. Frau Radenour will help thee and see that none cheat thee. Run now and ask if thou canst go with her." And Grandmother shut her eyes and lay back on her pillow.

Karen listened with her blue eyes wide open, for she had not known how close they were to want. Grandmother had never told her how little she had been able to save; and, any-way, Karen had but small idea of the value of money. But now she realized that they must be terribly poor, or Grandmother would never part with the brass candlesticks of which she had always been very proud. These were really beautiful in their simple but good design and their honest workmanship; both were ornamented with a pattern of beaten work, and with them went a tiny, pointed snuffer; they had been made by hand, long before, and had been in Grandmother's family for many generations. Grandmother prized the candlesticks very highly, and so did Karen, who knew how to polish them till they fairly shone. For even among the poorer folk of old Bruges many things of household use were made of brass or copper, and every one kept these things scoured and polished with the greatest care.

As Karen passed through the living-room on her way to ask Frau Radenour she looked at the treasured candlesticks shining from the dresser shelf, and the tears; filled her eyes just as they did Grandmother's, who was weeping quietly as she lay back in her bed.

In a few minutes Karen came back and told Grandmother that Frau Radenour would gladly take her along to the market and look after her, and that she must be ready to start in just a little while.

"Stay close to her, Karen," warned Grandmother, "and do with thy wares whatever way she thinks best, for she is a good bargainer and will see that thou art dealt with fairly. Now, bring the candlesticks for me to see them once more before thou must take them away."

As Karen, lifting them from the dresser, brought them to her bed, Grandmother's thin fingers caressed them lovingly; for both had belonged to her mother and her mother's mother before her, and were the most treasured of the few possessions she had hoped to hand down to Karen. But they must have bread; and so with a sigh presently she withdrew her hands and folded them over the coverlet.

Karen placed the candlesticks carefully in her blue apron, and, holding up its hem tightly in one hand, she kissed Grandmother and smoothed her covers, and then she went over to Frau Radenour's house and together they set out for the rag-market.

Bruges has always been a city of many kinds of markets; and this one whither they were going was held every week or two on an open plot of ground on the banks of one of the quiet old canals and near the Quai Vert. It was called the rag-market because there on the grass under the double row of gnarled chestnut trees, dealers and humble folk of the poorer class spread out their wares.

Some brought only rags; though oftentimes others, driven by want, offered for sale something really beautiful: perhaps a bit of lace or a piece of old copper or brass handed down, as were Karen's wares, from the days when the poorer people were less poor and when in the making of even the simplest things for use in their homes the workmen had put their loving thought and skill.

When Karen and Fran Radenour reached the place, a number of people were already there arranging the things they had brought. Fran Radenour, who often came to the market, knew almost everyone, and with a smile and a "good day!" to those about her, she chose a place and spread out the bits of cloth she had for sale. "Do thou sit down here beside me," she said kindly to Karen, "and place thy things so," and she pointed to a spot in front of them.

As Karen placed her precious candlesticks on the ground, the polished brass gleamed in the fresh green grass like a cluster of yellow crocuses. Karen's face looked like a little spring flower, too, only very pale, and her eyes had a pathetic droop, as she sat under the flickering shadows of the young chestnut leaves. The cap that covered her plaited hair was very stiff and white, and as she smoothed her little blue apron over the black dress she wore, she looked wonderingly around at the people who were beginning to loiter along the path between the trees and now and then to stop and price or perhaps buy some of the wares for sale.

Karen had once or twice before been to the rag-market with Grandmother; but that was to buy and not to sell, and she thought it a very different matter now.

Presently one, and then another woman stopped and looked at the candlesticks in front of Karen. But when they asked the price and Frau Radenour, who took charge of the matter, insisted on ten francs, they shook their heads and turned away. The poor little girl's eyes filled with tears, but Frau Radenour, who was a shrewd bargainer, said: "Cheer up, little one, thy wares are worth the price, and we will not give them to the first one who asks!"

Karen, though, was quite sure that no one else would come; and while she hated the thought of parting with the pretty candlesticks, neither did she wish to go back to Grandmother without carrying her the money, which she knew they must need so dreadfully. And so, that Frau Radenour might not see her tears, she turned away her face.

The sunlight glinting between the trees touched the quiet water of the canal near by and flecked it with silver. By the mossy piers of the picturesque old bridge that spanned it a family of black and white ducks were swimming about, every now and then dipping their broad, yellow bills into the water and spattering it in twinkling drops over their glossy feathers. And quite near to Karen a beautiful white swan drifted along arching her neck proudly and looking toward Karen as if she expected the happy smile and "Good day!" with which the little girl always greeted these stately white birds she so admired.

But poor Karen had no heart to talk to even her beloved swans; yet she put up her hand and brushed away the tears, and tried to be interested as Frau Radenour, after a little bargaining, sold her bits of cloth to a woman in a black dress with a fringed kerchief crossed over her shoulders. The woman was making a piece of rag carpet at home and needed a few more strips of cloth to finish it, and she found Frau Radenour's to her liking.

Just as the bargain was finished, a man came strolling along smoking a pipe. He seemed to have no special business there but just to smoke his pipe and enjoy the spring air as it blew softly between the chestnut trees. Now and then he stopped and glanced at some of the wares spread out for sale on either side of the path; but more often his eyes wandered down the length of the canal to a little gap between the brown roofs of the old houses that fringed its winding course. For through this little gap one could see the tall masts of a cluster of schooners moored at a quay beyond a not far distant bend.

The reason these interested the man more than anything else was because he was a sailor; and as his boat happened to be waiting for some cargo to be made ready, he was taking a little stroll in the meantime. But the reason that the sailor stopped still when he came to Frau Radenour and Karen, and looked hard at the little girl, was because he happened to be none other than Hans.

Now, Hans still had the little porringer, and though he had been back in Bruges several times since he went to live on Captain Helmgar's boat, he had not perhaps taken so much pains as he might to restore it. He had always meant to take it back, but always there was something to do that seemed to interfere, and perhaps, too, he had been almost glad of one excuse or another to delay returning it; for still the longer he had it, the more he hated to part with it. And, curiously enough, although he had stolen it, he somehow felt that if it had not been for it he would still be Robber Hans, and he found an honest life very much better and more agreeable than he had thought. And then, too, since he was leading a life in which he could respect himself once more, the memories which the porringer awakened no longer pained and angered him as they had done at first when he had tried to destroy it. For though he had thought then that it was with the porringer, it was really with himself that he had been angry, because he had made his life so worthless that he did not like to compare it with the happier days of his childhood that the porringer had recalled to him. But now he liked to look at it and think of the old Quiberon days; and still the little pictured face of Emschen smiled up at him from its bowl and spurred him on to do the best he could.

But though Hans still kept the porringer, he knew very well that he ought to return it to the little girl he had seen sweeping the steps of the yellow house on the corner; and notwithstanding he had delayed so long, he still honestly meant to try to find a chance to restore it to her.

Now, as he saw her sitting there on the grass beside Frau Radenour, he knew her at once, though he thought her face looked thinner and less rosy than when he had seen her before. As he stared at Karen, presently Frau Radenour looked up curiously at him, and "Good day, Ma'm!" said Hans awkwardly, taking the pipe from his mouth.

"Good day!" replied Frau Radenour, and Karen looked up, too. But though she half remembered Hans' face, she could not place him; for it had been only a minute or two that he had stopped at the doorstep that day he had spoken to her, and then he had looked much more closely at her than she at him.

"Hast thou something to sell?" asked Hans, looking down at the candlesticks still nestling in the grass in front of the little girl.

"Yes," spoke up Frau Radenour, "the price is ten francs for the pair, and any one can see that is little enough for them!"

"They are good work," said Hans, still awkwardly, as he stooped down and lifted them in his hands. And, indeed, Hans in his robber days had taken enough things to be a judge of values.

"Yes, sir," ventured Karen in a low voice, as he admired the candlesticks, "I think they are pretty, and we would not sell them only Grandmother is sick and we must have the money."

It was the first time Karen had spoken, and "Hush, child!" said Frau Radenour aside to her. "Let me manage the bargaining!"

But Hans had already set the candlesticks down, and was searching his pockets, his face red with confusion and mortification. He would have given anything to be able to buy them and at a much larger price than that asked, for he thought vaguely that he might thus make up to the little girl for having taken the porringer which of course was worth only a few sous. But he did not possess the ten francs! Again he felt desperately in his pockets, but scarcely half that sum was all he could muster.

The fact was Hans had not been wasting his earnings as a sailor, but had spent some of his first honest money to buy himself the decent clothes of which he was sorely in need; and then afterward he had used all he could spare to pay some old debts which he was ashamed to think had stood so long against him. His wages on the fishing vessel were not large, and so it had taken some time to do these things, and now barely five francs was all Hans possessed in the world.

As he thus stood confusedly, wishing with all his heart that he had more money to offer for the candlesticks, it happened that another man came along and began to look at them. This man was the owner of a little shop in the city and dealt in brass and copper wares, and he knew the rag-market and often picked up beautiful things very cheaply there; for the poor people who brought them for sale did not expect to receive the full value of their wares, but, pressed sharply by their need, had to be content to sell them for what they could.

As the dealer now examined Karen's candlesticks he quickly saw that they were of beautiful workmanship and that, as Frau Radenour declared, ten francs was little enough for them. But though he felt perfectly sure that he could sell them from his shop for a great deal more, he was unwilling to pay the ten francs until Frau Radenour had exhausted all her skill as a saleswoman. At last, slowly drawing the francs from his purse, he handed them over and carried off the candlesticks; and though Frau Radenour insisted that he had bought them for but half their value, she knew it was probably the best they could have hoped for in the rag-market.

While this chaffering was going on, Karen had sat mute and sad-eyed, and Hans, too, had not moved away, but still stood helplessly, not quite knowing what to do. But when the dealer had walked off, he drew a step nearer Karen, and, again turning very red with confusion, he extended to her his hand in which lay the five francs, and, "Little girl," he stammered, "won't you please take these? They are all I have."

At this Karen drew back timidly and looked up at him in bewilderment, while Frau Radenour stared with surprise. In a moment, however, the latter recovered herself and said, with a touch of sharpness in her voice, "Many thanks, sir, but keep your money; the child is no beggar!" Indeed, with the sturdy pride of the hard-working poor, Frau Radenour resented Hans' well-meant offer, and she knew, too, that Karen's Grandmother would be greatly displeased had she allowed Karen to accept the charity of a stranger.

But as she took the little girl's hand and they both rose to their feet and started off for home, she wondered over and over why the strange sailor had stared so at Karen and had wanted to give her all his money.

As they walked away, Hans, on his part, looked gloomily after them as he reluctantly replaced the five francs in his pocket.

He was deeply disappointed that he had not been able to give them to Karen, for he now realized that she and her Grandmother must be much poorer than he had supposed. The little yellow house looked comfortable, and better than those of most of the lace-makers, and Hans had not before thought that the two who lived there had found life a hard struggle.

As this began to sink into his mind he began to wake up. Indeed, Hans' better nature had been asleep so long while he was leading his evil life that it took quite a while for it to waken entirely; though every day for those three months past he had been rousing up more and more.

[58]

As he now turned again and strode along the path by the old canal, "What if it were Emschen?" he kept saying to himself. "She isn't even so big as Emschen was, and the Grandmother is sick and they have no one to work for them!" And then another idea came into the mind of Hans, and it interested him so that he forgot to finish smoking his pipe and he almost ran into a great, shaggy dog harnessed to a little cart full of brass milk cans.

"Look out!" cried the woman trudging along beside the cart. "Thou art a great clumsy fellow!"

And Hans, muttering a shame-faced apology, turned up a narrow street and made his way back to the quay where the fishing vessels were moored.

CHAPTER 7

GRANDMOTHER AND KAREN

WHEN Frau Radenour and Karen came back to The Little Street Of The Holy Ghost and drew near the corner where Karen lived, Frau Radenour, who had carefully carried the money for the candlesticks, now gave it to the little girl and with a cheery good-by went on to her own home.

Karen hurried up the steps and pushing open the door went into the room where Grandmother lay in her bed. Bending over her patient old face, she kissed her, and then laying the ten francs on the counterpane said, "See, Grandmother! Frau Radenour says this will keep us in bread for quite a long time! And you know we did not need the candlesticks."

Then Grandmother stroked Karen's hand and said: "Thou art a dear child, Karen, and thou hast done well. Grandmother is better now and we will get along."

She told Karen to go to a little shop not far away and buy them some food, of which they had but a scanty supply.

After their humble little dinner Grandmother felt so much better that she was able, with Karen's help, to put on her dress and sit by the open window for a while.

In a few days she had improved so much that she took up the lace-pillow again, and began work. Day by day, beneath her deft fingers, the delicate threads grew into white flowers and frosty tissues; and Karen, sitting by her side, learned to make a flower shaped like a little hyacinth bell, and Grandmother smiled proudly and said she would be a fine lacemaker. And then Karen tried harder than ever to learn how to use the tiny bobbins.

Sometimes, through the pleasant spring days, they sat on the doorstep and worked. There was a convent not far away where the nuns taught the children of the poorer folk of Bruges. And often, as Grandmother looked at Karen working so hard over her little black pillow, she grieved much that the little girl could not go to this school at least a part of every day, for she wanted her to have a chance to learn something; but she could not spare her. For though Grandmother was better, she was not strong and could not work so steadily as she had done before. Karen had to help as much as she could about the house and in every way relieve her, which kept the little girl busy.

Early in the summer Madame Koerner, who had returned from Ghent, had Karen come every afternoon to play with and look after her little boy, and, in this she earned a little money, till Madame Koerner was called away again.

But yet, in spite of all their efforts, Grandmother and Karen had hard work to keep themselves from want. And from time to time Grandmother's tired hands would tremble so she would have to stop work for a little while. And then Karen would have to go again to the rag-market with Frau Radenour and carry with her some one of their few possessions. In this way they parted with the little brass coffee-pot which, next to the candlesticks, had been the pride of Grandmother's heart; and then, later on, went a pitcher, and even Karen's pewter mug, and one or two pieces of the precious linen which Grandmother had tried to store up for the little girl against the time when she grew up and would perhaps have a home of her own.

So, gradually, the little house grew more and more bare within, though Grandmother and Karen still bravely struggled on, and in one way and another managed to keep from the almshouse.

But though the little girl had to work so hard, she had her simple little pleasures, too. Sometimes Grandmother finished her lace for some one of the ladies who had seen her work at Madame Koerner's and who lived in that part of the city. And then it was one of Karen's chief delights to take the work home; for she loved to walk through their gardens where old-fashioned roses and poppies and blue corn-flowers bloomed, and snapdragons and larkspurs and many other gay blossoms splashed their bright color along the box-bordered paths, for Bruges has always been famous for her beautiful flowers. And often when the little girl came home it would be with her hands full of posies that had been given her, and these brightened up the bare little house and helped make them forget the many things they had been obliged to part with. Though not all the flowers stayed within, for Karen always took pains to pick out the very prettiest one, and then with this in her hand she would lean from the sill of the window nearest the little shrine at the corner of the house, and there she would tuck the flower within the little hand of the Christ-child's image. For it did not seem to her fitting that the house should be decorated within and the shrine left bare.

Another thing Karen loved to do was to go with Grandmother, sometimes on Sunday afternoons when they had a holiday, out to the pretty little lake called the Minne-Water, which lay just within the old city walls. Here, where the great elm trees cast their dappled shadows, many white swans were always to be found floating about. Karen always saved part of her bread on Sundays that she might have the delight of feeding the lovely great birds, who would swim up as she leaned over the edge of the water and eat the morsels from her rosy palm.

Indeed, it takes but little to give pleasure when one works hard all week long. And as Karen bent over her lace-pillow day after day, she would dream about the gardens and the swans on the Minne-Water till sometimes she would drop her bobbins and tangle her thread, and Grandmother would have to bid her be more careful; and then she would set to work again and her little fingers would fairly fly.

Day by day, up in the wonderful belfry, the silvery chimes rang out the hours, till the summer had passed away and the autumn came. Soon the starlings and cuckoos all flew away to warmer lands, and in the open spaces of the city the green leaves of the chestnut trees curled up and fluttered down to the ground, and the great willows, that here and there overhung the old canals, slowly dropped their golden foliage to float away on the silvery water below.

In the little yellow house Grandmother and Karen now had to burn some of their precious hoard of wood even after their bit of cooking on the hearth was done; and Karen could no longer put a flower for the Christ-child up in the little shrine of the house.

Indeed, as winter drew on, bringing with it thoughts of the Christmas time, Karen said to herself sadly that this year she would have no money to spend for the little gifts she so loved to make. She remembered how pleased she had been the Christmas before to select and buy the green jug for Grandmother and the pretty porringer for the Christ-child. Grandmother had liked the jug as well as Karen had hoped she would; and she hoped, too, that the Christ-child had been pleased with the porringer—she was sure he had found it on the doorstep, because it was gone the next morning.

She wished she might buy presents for both of them again, but she knew that even if some of the ladies Grandmother worked for should give her a silver piece as had Madame Koerner the year before, she would have to spend it for the food they must have and for which it seemed so hard to get the money.

There was one thing though that, poor as they were, Grandmother felt they must provide against the Christmas time; they must have their wax candles to take to the cathedral even if they had to do without light themselves.

So when the time wore on and the day before Christmas came, just as they had done as far back as Karen could remember, they set out for the ancient cathedral, each carrying a white taper to be blessed and lighted and add its tiny golden flame to the hundreds twinkling through the dim, perfumed air.

When the vesper service was over, and again they walked slowly back to the little house, its steep roof was powdered over with light snowflakes that were beginning to pile up in soft drifts on the points of the gable and to flutter down to the street below.

As Karen looked up at the little shrine hung with its wintry fringe of twinkling icicles, and at the image of the Christ-child within, she wondered if the real Christ-child would bring her something again at midnight. And she wondered, too, for the thousandth time, how he could bring gifts to so many children in a single night, and how it was that he did not grow very tired and cold, as she was then, and she had been no farther than the cathedral.

But Grandmother said he did not feel the cold nor grow tired like other children so long as they kept him warm with their love; but that if he found a child whose heart was cold and who did not try to obey him, then he shivered in the snow and his little feet grew so weary! Karen could not see how any child could help loving him when he was so good to them all; and she wished again that she had some little gift to show him that she thought about him, and cared for him.

She gave a little sigh as they went in, but soon she was busy helping set out their supper, and then when they had finished, and put the dishes back on the dresser, she and Grandmother sat by the hearth in the flickering light of the fire.

And as they looked into the embers, they both saw visions and dreamed dreams. Grandmother's dreams were of long ago, when Karen's mother was a little girl like Karen herself; while Karen dreamed of the time when she would be grown up and able to do wonderful things for Grandmother.

CHAPTER 8

CHRISTMAS EVE AGAIN

As Grandmother and Karen still sat in the firelight, dreaming their dreams and thinking of many things, not far away, along The Little Street Of The Holy Ghost, a man was walking rapidly. Of course there was nothing odd about that, but it *was* curious that this man was the very same one who had hurried down that very street exactly a year before—and yet any one who had seen him then would never have believed that it could possibly be the same.

For instead of Hans the Robber, unkempt and ragged, walking stealthily and keeping a constant sharp lookout lest he be surprised in some of his evil doing, this man Hans was decently clad and bore himself fearlessly. He carried something in his hands, and he seemed to be looking for some place.

Presently he came to the corner where stood the little yellow house, and there he paused for a moment and a look of disappointment came into his face; for there seemed to be no light in the house and it looked as if no one were home. But as Hans came opposite to one of the little windows, he glanced in and could see Grandmother and Karen sitting hand in hand by the hearth. Then he looked carefully about him and noticed across the street a narrow passageway that lay in the shadow between two rambling old houses, and he gave a little smile of satisfaction.

The next thing he did was to place the objects he had been carrying in his hands in a row on the doorstep, close in front of the door, so that any one opening it could not help but see them—that is, if the room within had been light, for otherwise the deep, old-fashioned doorway was quite in shadow. There was no street lamp near, and, though the snow had ceased, the night was moonless and the stars partly hidden by clouds. A few lights shone faintly from some of the houses opposite, but these did not help any, as they did not touch the doorstep; and as Hans realized that the things he had placed there could thus scarcely be seen, he looked troubled for a moment, but suddenly he broke into a low laugh as he said to himself: "Lucky I thought to put in candles!"

And then, fumbling in his pockets, at last he found a bit of paper which had been wrapped around his tobacco; for his pipe was the one indulgence that Hans allowed himself, and this he seldom left behind if he could help it. Having found the bit of paper, he hastily twisted it into a tiny taper, and then he looked up and down the street to be sure it was quite deserted, for he wanted to have things to himself for a few minutes.

There was no one in sight, and he could hear no footfalls; so quickly thrusting the taper into the bowl of his pipe, he held his hand around it and blew softly on the glowing coals till in a moment the taper caught fire. Then, instantly, he stooped and laid it to the tips of two tall, shimmering white objects in the row he had set on the step, and which proved to be candles held in a pair of brass candlesticks. Hans had little trouble in lighting them, for the air was perfectly still and the space in front of the door deep enough to shelter the candles well. When the tiny golden flames sprang up, they showed that between them on the step was what seemed to be a little bowl with blue handles, only instead of being full of sweetmeats, as one might perhaps expect on Christmas eve, it was filled with something that glistened with a silvery light.

But Hans did not stop to look at these things, for the moment the candles began to burn he gave a knock on the door, and then, quick as a flash, he darted across the narrow street, and drew back in the dark shadow of the passageway he had noticed. For, while he did not wish to be seen, he wanted to watch and be sure that the things he had brought were safely received and not stolen by some night prowler such as he himself had been a year before.

Hans had scarcely hidden himself when he heard Karen tugging to unbar the door; and, in another moment, as she pulled it open, he saw her stand perfectly still in the golden candlelight, clasping her hands in utter amazement, while the startled wonder grew in her blue eyes as she stared down at the things at her feet.

Then presently, "Grandmother! Grandmother!" she cried excitedly in a high, sweet voice, "come quickly and see what the Christ-child has brought!"

Hans could see Grandmother hurry to Karen as the little girl knelt on the floor and lifting up the lighted candles exclaimed, "Look, Grandmother! Here are Christmas candles in our very own brass candlesticks!"

And then as Grandmother, speechless with amazement, took the candles from her and Karen lifted up the dish that had stood between them, "Why—why, it is full of silver *money!*" she cried in bewilderment; and then, as she looked at the blue handles and the stripe of color around its edge, she exclaimed, "And oh, Grandmother, I do believe this is the very porringer I gave the Christ-child last Christmas!"

She rose to her feet and carried the porringer over to the table where Grandmother had already set the candles, and Hans heard no more.

Indeed, at that moment Hans was standing up very straight with a startled look growing on his own face, and with Karen's words still ringing in his ears.

"What?" he repeated to himself. *"The very porringer she gave the Christ-child?"* and he began to think very hard.

In a moment it all straightened itself out in his mind. Hans drew a deep breath, and then he said to himself slowly: "So that was why it was outside on the doorstep! And it was no gift some one had brought *her*—but a present from her to the *Christ-child!*—And—and—*I* took it!" And Hans gasped and turned pale; for even in his worst robber days he would as soon have thought of stealing something from the cathedral as the Christ-child's porringer, had he known what it was.

"And to think," he went on to himself, with a horrified look in his face, "that I tried to break it, and to sell it at the *thieves' market*, and then kept it all this while—and *what if I had not brought it back!"* Here Hans fairly shivered with fear; for he felt that he had been guilty of a particularly dreadful sin when he took that little porringer, and he began to wonder what punishment he would receive for it.

But all at once he heard Karen's happy laughter ring out from the little house, for in their excitement the door still stood partly open. And then a ray of light from a lamp in one of the brown houses beside him shone out through a window, and, crossing the narrow street, touched the front of the little yellow house, and wavered, and presently flitted for a moment into the little shrine up in the corner; and, as Hans looked, it beamed over the face of the Christ-child, who seemed to be

[69]

gazing down right into the eyes of Hans and smiling happily. And at that moment, Hans could not have told why, but all his fear vanished and he began to smile happily himself.

As he came from his hiding-place and started off briskly down the street, and up in the beautiful belfry the chimes played sweetly through the frosty air, he found himself whistling softly a little tune keeping time with the bells; and he knew his heart had not been so light since he was a little boy in Quiberon.

CHAPTER 9

KAREN PERPLEXED

W HILE Hans went thus whistling happily down the street, Grandmother and Karen were still breathless with excitement over the good fortune that had come to them.

With trembling hands Grandmother had emptied the contents of the porringer on the table, and as she looked at the little pile of shining silver coins that had filled it she knew it was enough to keep them for months—yes, with their simple wants, they might live on it for a year! And already she felt stronger and better able to work since the fear of the almshouse was thus gone—at least for a long while.

But *where* had the money come from? She stood dazed before it, so bewildered trying to account for it that presently Karen asked her in surprise, "Why, Grandmother, wasn't it the Christ-child who brought everything?" And then she answered slowly and softly, with awe and wonder quivering through her voice, "Yes, little one, it must have been none other than the Christ-child!"

And, of course, it was; and that he had chosen Hans to be his messenger was quite his own affair. If the little silver coins could have spoken, they might have told Grandmother and Karen how Hans had saved them one by one. Indeed, it was less than a week after he had seen Karen selling the candlesticks in the rag-market that he had been offered a place as sailor on a large vessel about to start on a voyage to far-away China; and Captain Helmgar, though sorry to part with him, had been glad of his good luck, for Hans was really a fine sailor and he could earn better wages on the larger vessel. And so it was that the first silver pieces found themselves put into a little bag, and every month more and more coming to keep them company. They might have told, too, how on ship-board Hans was called a miser, because when the vessel anchored at strange cities he spent nothing for amusements and the things which sailors usually like to do when on land; and how Hans, though he hated to be thought stingy, had yet smiled to himself the larger his hoard grew; for he knew very well that he was really no miser and that he had his own reasons for saving the silver pieces.

And then, if the candlesticks could have talked, they might have taken up the story and told how, when a certain large vessel from China had moored at Ostend the week before, a sailor named Hans had come back to Bruges and had inquired if they were still in the shop of the dealer he had seen buying them in the rag-market. And how he had spent just enough from his bag-full of silver to buy them and take them away from the shelf where they had stood so long because the dealer, a grasping man, had set so high a price that no one would buy; and so at last when Hans offered him a fair sum he was glad enough to sell them. And then they could have told how he had gone to the Christmas market in the Grande Place and bought the two white candles.

And, last of all, the little porringer might have finished the tale by saying: "I was really the one, you know, that started it all; for Hans used often to look at me, and my little girl with the rose in her hand—he called her Emschen—used to smile at him, and always reminded him of Karen and how Karen

[72]

needed some one to help her, and how I really belonged to her,—for he did not know then that she had bought me for the Christ-child. At any rate, he kept saving the silver just so he could fill my bowl with them and bring me back to Karen, and so here I am!"

But though, if they could have spoken, they might have told all these things to Grandmother and Karen, the Christmas candles contented themselves with filling their little flames with golden light, and the candlesticks just shone and twinkled, and the silver coins gleamed softly, and the little girl in the porringer seemed fairly to laugh with glee as Karen looked into her face.

As for Karen, she was so delighted with it all that she danced about the room like a little mad-cap sprite. But though her heart was brimming over with happiness, there was one thing that perplexed her: while she knew perfectly well that their good fortune had come from the Christ-child, she could not understand why he had brought back the porringer. With the other things it was different, for, of course, he knew how they had hated to part with the candlesticks and how much they needed the money; but the porringer had been meant all the while for him, and so why had he brought it back?

Grandmother, who had never seen it before, listened in bewilderment as Karen, standing beside the table, now told her about buying it for the Christ-child and leaving it on the doorstep the year before; and she scarcely knew what to say when, with a troubled look, the little girl asked: "Do you think he did not like it, Grandmother?"

Grandmother was silent a moment, and then, "No, child," she answered, "else why would he have filled it with silver and stood it between the lighted candles? No, he must have

[73]

had some reason we do not understand, but I feel sure he was pleased with it."

Karen thought very hard for a few minutes, and at last she said: "I think he must have brought it back because he knew we had to sell my pewter mug, and that I have only the cup with the broken handle for my bread and milk."

Karen was very well satisfied with this explanation, but somehow she felt that having meant it as a present for the Christ-child she did not want to take the porringer back; and so she hardly knew what to do with it. But in a moment she looked up with a happy smile, and "Oh, Grandmother," she exclaimed, "I thought what to do with it! I will put it up in the little shrine, so if he wants it again he can find it!"

Grandmother thought that would be a very nice thing to do with the porringer; and as the Christmas candles slowly burned away, they sat there talking over the wonderful thing that had happened to them, till it seemed like some marvellous dream, and they would have to rub their eyes and look again and again at the little porringer, and the silver coins, and the white candles tipped with golden flame, to be quite sure that it was all really true.

CHAPTER 10

THE PORRINGER FINDS A RESTING-PLACE

AND if Grandmother and Karen were radiant with happiness that Christmas eve, not less so was Hans the sailor. And on Christmas morning, when all the bells of Bruges pealed out their glad carillons, instead of filling his heart with bitterness as they had done a year before when he sat by his desolate hearth in the forsaken hut, now they sounded sweet and joyous in his ears, and he thought the world a fine and pleasant place to live in after all. And above all he was glad and thankful that the porringer was safely back. But although he had restored it to Karen, he had become so interested in her that he did not mean to lose sight of her; nor did he.

He continued to be a sailor on the large ship, and voyaged to and fro over the sea, but whenever he was on shore he always looked up the little yellow house and tried to learn how life fared with Grandmother and Karen. Before long he found means to become acquainted with them, and in many ways, often unknown to themselves, he befriended them.

But as time went on, he wanted to do more. To be sure, the silver coins he had put in the porringer had brought to the two warmth and light and food and comfort, such as they had not known for many a month; and Grandmother had still been able to lay aside quite a sum of money against a rainy day; and the knowledge that they had this nest-egg to fall back on if either fell ill again brought relief and peace of mind that only those who have struggled for their bread can fully know. And it was with a lighter heart than she had had for years that Grandmother still kept on with her lace-making; and day, by day, sitting beside her, still Karen tried her best to master the beautiful art.

But whenever Sailor Hans came to see them it distressed him to find them toiling over the little black pillows, and to feel that he himself had no one to do for and yet was so much better able to work than they. For during those months that Hans had saved up the silver coins for the porringer he had made a discovery, and that was that it was very much pleasanter and happier to have some object in life and some one to work for.

But whenever he strove to help them, Grandmother's pride forbade, for, of course, she knew no reason why he should do so. So at last one day Hans quietly told her the story of his life; and, in so doing, to the surprise of both of them, they discovered that Grandmother had known and loved his own mother in their girlhood days in Bruges.

When Hans had finished, he begged Grandmother for the sake of this friendship, and most of all because of what Karen had unwittingly done for Hans himself, that she would let him care for them as if she were his own mother and Karen his own little long-lost sister Emschen; and he begged so earnestly that Grandmother, with all her pride, could no longer refuse, and when she gave her consent nothing had ever made Hans more proud and happy.

From his monthly earnings he began regularly to set aside a certain sum to go to the little yellow house. Often, too, from his voyages he brought back some foreign gift for Grandmother or pretty trinket for Karen; and once, oddly enough, it was a little string of coral beads, so much prettier than the blue ones she had so longed for that day she bought the porringer in the Christmas market that she laughed with delight, and flinging her arms around his neck, she kissed Hans and declared he was the best friend she had!

Sometimes when he was on shore in summer, he would come up to the little yellow house and Grandmother would sit in the open doorway with her lace-pillow in her lap—for he could not persuade her to give up her work entirely—while Karen and he sat on the doorstep, the little girl industriously working, too. And then Hans, soberly smoking his pipe, would tell Karen every little while that she must not hurt her eyes, as she must save them for the time when she went to school. For one of the first things that Hans had seen to was to arrange for Karen to go to the convent school where Grandmother had wished to send her. And then Karen would laugh and say: "I will just finish this one lace flower, Sailor Hans, and then I will stop."

And always from the little shrine up in the corner of the house the Christ-child nestling on his mother's breast seemed to smile down at them with a wise look in his baby eyes, while down at the edge of Mother Mary's blue robe gleamed the blue handles of the little porringer.

Sometimes, when Karen had a flower, she filled the porringer with fresh water and placed the flower within it. And one day the pigeons found it out, and, fluttering down from the steep roofs near by, came to drink from it. Karen, seeing this with delight, always after took pains every day to fill it freshly from the wonderful dragon pump, so that the pigeons might not be disappointed. And it was a pretty sight to see them one at a time poising at the edge of the shrine and bending their glossy necks to dip up the water.

When winter came and the icicles hung their rainbow fringe from the carved canopy above, and the white hoar-frost wreathed the little bowl and trailed from the blue handles like garlands of fairy flowers, then Karen filled it every day with crumbs. For Sailor Hans, for some reason she never knew, always took a great interest in the porringer, and always left a little piece of silver to supply it; and whenever Christmas time came he insisted that it must be kept heaped with barley, so that the birds might have a holiday feast.

And by and by, when Grandmother had come to take life more easily and sometimes folded the patient hands that had wrought so many exquisite things, when Karen had grown a tall girl, sweet and helpful, still filling the little house with happy laughter and with the dreams in her blue eyes growing deeper and deeper, when their staunch friend Hans was no longer sailor but grey-haired Captain Hans, honored and respected by all who knew him, still the little porringer stood in the shrine. And through summers and winters the birds ate and drank from it, and the Christ-child seemed quite content that it should stay there.

This was all many years ago; but unless he has taken it away, no doubt it is still standing in the spot chosen by Karen, close by the feet of Mother Mary and watched over by the Holy Babe she clasps so lovingly to her heart.

END

CPSIA information can be obtained
at www.ICGtesting.com
Printed in the USA
LVHW091109031120
670569LV00004B/549